We
OVERCOME

We OVERCOME

Demecia Lewis

XULON PRESS

Xulon Press
2301 Lucien Way #415
Maitland, FL 32751
407.339.4217
www.xulonpress.com

Unless otherwise indicated, Scripture quotations taken
from the King James Version (KJV) – *public domain*.

Scripture quotations taken from the Holy Bible, New
International Version (NIV). Copyright © 1973, 1978,
1984, 2011 by Biblica, Inc.™. Used by permission. All
rights reserved.

Printed in the United States of America.

Paperback ISBN-13: 978-1-63221-831-5
eBook ISBN-13: 978-1-6322-1832-2

DEDICATION

I dedicate this book to my Lord and Savior Jesus Christ, who is faithful to His word. His love is everlasting, His promises are true, and His grace is sufficient and new every morning.

PROLOGUE

"And they overcame him by the blood of the Lamb and by the word of their testimony. And they did not love their lives so much that they were afraid to die" (Rev. 12:11).

WE OVERCOME SATAN BY THE BLOOD OF the lamb, and by the words of our testimony. Testimonies are powerful; they ignite the faith of those in despair and need, and remind us that there are possibilities for deliverance, breakthrough, promotion, and healing. God's word says, "if He did it for one, He can surely do the same for you." God is not a respecter of persons; He is a just and sovereign God. A Father, all-knowing, he desires to bless you with your heart's desires. Testimonies spark glimmers of hope in areas that once appeared hopeless. Beloved, every season can change. So, I encourage you to not ever allow your adversary to derail the assignments that God has specifically ordained for you. Zech. 4:10 admonishes us to despise not the days of small beginnings. Often, during stagnant or unfruitful seasons, when things do not develop as fast as we think they should (business, relationships, etc.), at the slightest hint of adversity, we allow doubt, uncertainty, and discouragement to creep in. When these dispiriting feelings hang around long enough, another evil can enter, its name, **fear**.

Fear can be daunting to overcome. But remember, God has not given us the spirit of fear, but that of the powers of both love and a sound mind (2 Tim. 1:7-9). To rise above these things, Beloved, you must have faith that what God promised you will come to pass.(Hab. 2:3 gives a firm promise of this: "for the vision is yet for an appointed time, but at the end, it shall speak and not lie: though it tarries, wait for it; because it will surely come, it will not tarry.")

In this book, you will read testimonies from the hearts of those who believed God during times of uncertainty, who were delivered from alcoholism, pornography, drugs, homelessness, prostitution, domestic abuse and so much more. I believe their testimonies will awaken hope in you and encourage your faith that God will do just what he promised. I trust God that you did not choose this book by chance. I stand boldly on God's Word, and with absolute assurance that His word will work for you, allowing you to gain a fresh zeal, and renewed faith to believe Him for the impossible. He can grant you freedom from addictions, broken-heartedness, loneliness, grief, poverty, debt, sickness, depression, mental illnesses, perversion, generational curses and so much more. Not another day will you believe the father of lies. I declare and decree as a born-again believer that the very thing you need from God will manifest in your life in this season, that you will pass your test, and that you will testify that God did it for you. Do not lose heart! You have the power, as a believer, to command those threats and concerns to be thwarted; in the name of Jesus, you will overcome by the blood of the lamb and by the words of your testimony.

TABLE OF CONTENTS

Chapter 1

GOD MADE IT CLEAR

God's Vessel: Pastor Christopher Gregory

MY NAME IS CHRISTOPHER GREGORY, AND my wife's name is Calandra. We were high school sweethearts, have been married for 23 years (as of 2019), and have seven wonderful children aged between five and twenty-two. We both received Christ as our Lord and Savior within one year of marriage, and our commitment to serving Him at the time was marrow deep. I had begun reading the bible to live it, and came across a scripture that said, " … eye hath not seen, nor ear heard, neither have entered into the heart of man, the things which God hath prepared for them that love Him (1 Cor. 2:9, KJV)." I recall reading this scripture in our home in Albuquerque, New Mexico in early 1997 and being impressed with the idea that God had plans for me that (in our English vernacular) I had not even dreamed of. Often, when we consider the will of God, it seems like some elusive thing. I have spoken to people who are so afraid that they will "miss" the will of God. Others are frustrated because they are not sure what the will of the Lord is for their lives. I admit that I too had temporarily fallen into this crowd, but I pray that our testimony encourages you.

Our testimony is that God has made Himself clear to us as we have made our love, devotion, and commitment to Him clear in our lives. Notice that I did not say that I knew exactly what God wanted me to do all the time, only that the Lord was clear to us. When a baby sees its parents, the troubles that it has seem to grow dimmer. When Peter saw Jesus walk on water, suddenly, how to walk on water or what was going to hold him up in the water did not matter. For us, we simply were clear on the fact that we had our eyes on the Lord, and that if we stumbled, He was able to keep us from falling, rather than allow us to fail because I "missed something". He was able to joyously present me faultless before Himself! There are some major milestones where I have experienced Him guide us toward His will in this manner. In late 2002, I was within a few months of completing my bachelor's degree and pursuing my dream of becoming the first military officer in my family. I had served nine years in the United States Air Force, won numerous non-commissioned officer awards, did very well on the officer qualification test, and received glorious endorsements from my superiors. Everything was falling into place. It was during this time that the Lord had been impressing upon me His calling for my life to preach the gospel. As I committed to, and served faithfully in my local church, lived a holy life, and stayed content with my situation, I became increasingly aware that something was shifting. I began to realize that the Lord wanted me to forgo a military career for His calling of preaching the gospel. My wife and I talked, there were several spiritual friends with whom we shared our thoughts, and I also spoke with my pastor and leadership staff about what I was thinking. To muddy the water a little, around this time, we had two children and almost no savings. My wife became pregnant with twins and the military was offering me a bonus to reenlist which amounted to nearly $50,000. To make matters worse, the job market in Colorado Springs was not great. Through prayer with, and counsel from spiritual friends and our pastoral leadership, we made the faith move and declared to the Air Force that I would not reenlist. This decision was hastened by the fact that the Air Force had sent orders to report to Osan Air Base in South Korea in December of 2003. That was the end of my dream. With one signature, I turned down not only an assignment, but a dream that I had spent the previous 5 years thinking about, praying about, and working toward. I received this word from the Lord in my spirit during this season, "you want to be an officer in the military, but I am making you an officer in my army." God was so faithful to expunge the disappointment that I would have very naturally felt by reestablishing my thought process. Prov. 16:3 says, "Commit thy works unto the LORD, and thy thoughts shall be established (KJV)." During this time, we learned that we were pregnant with twins, so we took the little money that we had and used it as earnest money to start construction on a new home for when we separated from the military. Even as I write, I am shaking my head at how crazy that time was, and yet, I do not recall living in a constant state of worry or fear. I do recall nights when fear and anxiety would engulf me. There were times when I would look over at my wife (getting bigger by the day with the twins) and the enemy would tell me things like, "you are going to be homeless and your kids won't have anywhere to live", or "you are broke, what kind of man doesn't take care of his family?" or one of my favorites, "Go back and tell the Air Force you made a mistake and beg them to take you back." The only way I can describe the fear and anxiety that would descend on me each time the enemy's voice perked up is like a blanket, slowly limiting my ability to breathe. A pastor in our church had preached about Jehoshaphat recently. Jehoshaphat was a good king of Judah who was facing insurmountable odds against an army that was on the way to attack him. I was struck by the story because the scripture says that Jehoshaphat fasted and prayed, but it says that all Judah stood with their wives and children. I saw myself in Jehoshaphat. Jehoshaphat cried and remained steadfast unto the Lord, and his prayers began to be my combat weapon against the blanket of fear and anxiety that would descend upon me at night. This specific prayer stood out to me, "For we have no might to stand against this great company that is coming against us. We do not know what to do, but our eyes are upon You (2 Chron. 20:12, AMP)." This was my exact plight then: I had done all that I knew to do, I had made the necessary steps to get out of the military, I had applied for jobs all over, but no jobs were opening for me, my wife was getting bigger, and my separation date was getting closer. The final twist in all of this was, I felt very strongly to start my master's degree, so I began the enrollment process as well. As my closing date for the house approached, the mortgage company wanted to see that I had secured employment. I had not. They set certain timelines stating that if I had not secured by said date, they would have to rescind their financing. I had already missed a couple of those arbitrary deadlines, but I received a call stating that after a certain date, their decision would be final. My separation date was October 19th, 2003 and this 'drop dead' date was, if I recall correctly, about three weeks before that. I am so grateful to the close circle of friends that encouraged us during this time. Your faith walk often will not be for public consumption, because most times, it would seem unwise at best, and downright ridiculous at worst, to people who are not accustomed to walking by faith. These people prayed for us and reminded us of the promises of God and were simply whom God created them to be. All of this came to a head around late September/early October when a government contractor offered me a job doing almost the same thing I had been doing in the military. On October 1st, our twins were born, on October 3rd, I started a Master's degree, the week of October 13th, we moved into our new home, I drove off the base for the last time as active-duty personnel on October 19th, and drove back on October 20th as a contractor making almost twice the money I was making the day before. God had done it. He took my dreams and placed it on His potters' wheel and formed it into what He wanted. I never would have dreamed of living in Colorado, owning my own home with a wife and four kids (at the time), and working as a defense contractor for NORAD at one of the most critical times in our nation's history, all while preparing to go and pastor a church in two and a half years. During this time, I served over thirty general officers, worked with the White House, met, and spoke with the president, and learned a great deal about life, serving God and resting in His faithfulness. When it was time to leave this prestigious position to move to Phoenix as a pastor, the decision was not so hard, because we had been this way before. God had changed our thoughts to align with His will. We had never thought of or even dreamed of living in Arizona, but God had it pre-pared for us because we love Him. We had always said we would never move back to Alabama. I love my state, I just never wanted to live there again. It never entered our hearts that we would someday live in Alabama, much less love to live there. Guess where we now love to live?

When it comes to the will of God, the best thing you can do is be faithful where you are. I love what Calandra says, "live while you are living." She also says most people make more plans to get old and die than they do to live. We have learned to live as unto the Lord, and He has been faithful to guide us to the place where we need to be. So, do not let the devil discourage you. Get busy doing what you know you should be doing, and watch God do what only He can do!

Author's Comments

What a powerful testimony! I could not tear my eyes away, there were absolutely some key points that stand out that I believe we can all benefit from. Pastor Gregory and his wife, Calandra's decision to receive salvation automatically put them on the winning team in the first instance, and because they had become married believers, they then had double power. (One can send a thousand demons to flight, but two can send ten thousand to flight.)

Pastor Gregory sought God's word. He wanted to know the Lord so much, he consumed himself in His word. Even more so, he believed and trusted God's word. He served faithfully, walking in complete faith, even when his sight told him otherwise. He chose to not look at his situation in a natural way. He had to look at it spiritually, by faith, because he knew that the ways of God are not the ways of man. Through all this, they had friends who encouraged them, counselled them, and prayed for them.

Beloved, when you must make decisions like this, there is no better way to get a blessed outcome than by trusting God fully. Another thing to remember is to apply works to your faith. Pastor Gregory did not sit idle and pray as he believed God. No. He was busy seeking, working, and praying. He moved: he applied for jobs and enrolled for his masters. I'm so proud of my brother and I certainly appreciate him sharing this testimony with the world so that you too can overcome the enemy by the blood of Jesus, and so that your testimony will be the spark that ignites another man's faith to believe God when things don't look too believable.

Reflection

1. In addition to the below, can you list 5 other factors that worked for the Gregorys?

   a. Pastor Gregory always sought out and obeyed the directions of the Holy Spirit, even when he was not sure about how things would work out.

   b. He had a beautiful relationship with his wife, which made communication between them extremely easy, and both were believers who loved and believed in Jesus Christ.

   c. The Gregorys listened whenever God spoke to them. Pastor Gregory mentioned that he did not always know what God wanted him to do, only that he was clear that He wanted them to do something, and without hesitation, they obeyed each time.

   d. Gregorys' unwavering trust and love for God were second to none, and their obedience paid off.

   e. Pastor Gregory was aligned with the Holy Spirit and he always prayed and committed his trials to God in times of trouble.

2. Do you see anything in Pastor Gregory's testimony that can help you in your season of trials? If so, please list each one in addition to those below for your personal use.

   a. Faith, trust, and love of God are the key things I need to get me through my season of trials.
   b. Prayer and communion with the Holy Spirit are necessary for one's spiritual growth.
   c. Keeping friends whose interests resonate with mine, and who love and worship God as much as I do, are important so I can always have a shoulder to lean on, and exchange words of encouragement with them.

Chapter 2

ANOTHER NEGATIVE STATISTIC

God's Vessel: Isha V. Odom

MY NAME IS ISHA ODOM. I WAS BORN AND raised in the Tidewater area in Virginia. I would like to share a brief portion of my testimony. I was a teenage mom, was a high school drop-out, and lived in poverty. There are many angles to this testimony, however, I am going to share the short version.

My entire life, it did not seem like I would amount to much. Like many people, my vision was based on my environment—it was limited. By all accounts, I was headed to be another negative statistic. Trust me, there were lots of background noise and mistakes that were designed to keep me derailed and living low. Through many trials & tribulations, encouragement from some, and criticism from others, God changed my life! I will not say that it was easy, a 3-step system, or an event. It was a process and recognizing pivotal moments before my life began to change. So, do not be tempted to bypass the process, or curse the moments as they all catalyze your destiny.

Today, I serve as a senior leader alongside my husband at Agape Christian Worship Center located in Albany, Georgia. Currently, I own two businesses (I am a serial entrepreneur) and have earned my graduate degree in Public Administration. Recently, I became a certified speaker, coach, and trainer with the John Maxwell Team. This has opened doors for me to facilitate leadership and professional development training for the federal government, as well as for companies in the private sector. I also spend significant amounts of time sharing the gospel and empowering women. What does this mean? It means that you may begin rough, but if you stay the course, God can move in and transform your life. Do not allow people, obstacles, or even your limiting thoughts to serve as a hindrance. If one person could overcome their circumstances, you can too! God is no respecter of people; however, He requires faith and perseverance. You have everything you need because according to 2 Pet. 1:3, "His divine power has given us everything we need for living a godly life through our knowledge of Him who called us by His glory and goodness." (NIV)

Author's Comments

What an awesome testament to the faithfulness of God! I know Isha Odom personally and have felt firsthand the oil on her life as she has unselfishly bestowed blessings to my family in so many ways, especially in my years as a new mother in faraway Japan. I am beyond grateful for her sharing so freely with me her nuggets of wisdom and time-saving healthy recipes. I would not have known about the hardships and trials she endured, had she not shared them. God covered her. Some of the key points I believe we all can apply in our own lives from Isha's messages are as follows. Be sure to write down key points that stand out for you.

1. Be willing to go through the process, we must understand that this kind of success did not happen overnight.
2. Receive words of encouragement from others.
3. Let criticism drive you. Isha used the negative voices as fuel to succeed, even though it was not apparent to her at the time that she was using them as fuel—often, hindsight is 20/20. When we are ridiculed and judged, we can use that as a steppingstone. Have you ever heard the tale of the Donkey in the Well? One day, a farmer's donkey fell into a well. Being that the donkey was old and the

well needed to be filled anyway, the farmer decided it was easier to fill the well with dirt rather than to retrieve the donkey from it. So, he called neighbors over, and together, they tossed dirt in the well, intending to fill it with sand, thus, burying the donkey. The donkey cried horribly when it realized what was happening. When the dirt hit its back, it instinctively shook it off and took a step up. This process continued until the donkey was able to step up over the edges of the well, and happily trotted off. Beloved, life is going to shovel dirt on you, all kinds. It may manifest in the form of heartache, addictions, disappointments, or sicknesses. The key to overcoming all of it is to shake it off and take a step up. Shake it off by continuing to move. Do not lay dormant and allow yourself to be consumed by it. If Isha had not continued to move, work, believe, and persevere, she would have simply been another negative statistic. You cannot inherit accolades of that magnitude or get it by sitting where you are. She attended classes, studied, labored, and because she has a covenant with the Most High God, He has been faithful in His promises to prosper her and give her hope and a future. Recall that in Jer. 29:11, the Lord declared to each of us, "I know the plans I have for you. Plans to prosper you and not harm you. Plans to give you hope and a future". So, my dear brethren, stay the course, persevere, work hard, and never waver in your faith because with God, all things are possible (Matt. 19:26).

Chapter 3

I SHOULD HAVE DIED, BUT GOD SAID NO

God's Vessel: Lonnie Robinson

I AM 65 YEARS OLD. I HAVE BEEN HOME-less with an addiction both to crack cocaine and alcohol. I was savagely beaten, stabbed in the head with a hatchet, shot, struck by lightning, and badly mistreated for an awfully long time. I can count at least 6 different times in my life that I should have died but each time, God said no!

I was an alcoholic for 35 years (since I was 13!), a crack-cocaine addict for 15 years, helpless, hope-less, and homeless for 10 years. For 5 years, I slept on the streets of Miami and underneath the bridges, followed by another 5 years of sleeping in an aban-doned house. I used to "dumpster-dive". That is, eat food from the large garbage cans and dumpsters behind fast-food restaurants and supermarkets. I hit rock bottom and was literally on the cusp of death while I laid on the floor of that abandoned house,

surrounded by solid and liquid human waste. My
cardiovascular and respiratory systems were beginning to fail me, and, out of fear of being found
dead like that, I desperately sought God with all
my heart, mind, body, and soul. I knew (from my
friend) that the only way to get God to work in my
life would be to go through Lord Jesus. Therefore,
I crawled to my knees and cried out to Jesus, begging Him to save me.

After praying for a few nights without seeing
any signs that God had heard my cries, I felt Him!
He woke me up in the middle of the night and saved
me! I knew it was God because I always went into
the abandoned house at night, drunk and feeling bad,
with headaches and stomach aches, feeling miserable. But after God visited me, I felt brand new.

I thanked God all through that night, and early
that morning, I went to the grocery store where
I would usually beg for drinks each morning
to get my shakes off—my hands would shake
uncontrollably until I had enough alcohol in my
system. On this morning, Mr. Ralph, a regular
sponsor of my addiction, offered me a dollar to go
buy myself a beer as he always did each morning.
But I did not accept the dollar this time! Thank you,
Jesus!!! That was the first time in my life, since I
began drinking at the age of 13, that I turned down
an offer from anyone who wanted to buy/give me
a drink! Mr. Ralph asked me, "what about your
shakes?" I laid my hands out in front of Mr. Ralph

and let him see that my hands were just as steady as a surgeon in the operating room. I told Mr. Ralph that for several nights, I had been crying out to God to save me, and God heard my cries and He saved me! That morning, I went to "Better Way of Miami", a residential drug & alcohol rehabilitation facility for homeless people, and I have not had a drink or drug since that day, and it has been 16 years! Glory be to God!!

I turned my life and will over to the care of God, and the devil's bondage that I was wrapped up in lost its hold over me! God has miraculously transformed my life most profoundly! I am now 65 years old, and I have not had a drink or drug since that day, 16 years ago! I have been given "a clean bill of health" by my doctors at The Miami Veterans Hospital. I have never been helpless, hopeless, or homeless since that day, 16 years ago. I give God all the praise and glory; without Him, I am nothing, but with Him in my life, I am victorious! I am a winner!

After I graduated from the "Better Way of Miami" drug treatment program, I got a good job as a security officer supervisor (Lieutenant) for a large security company with government contracts, given my experience as a Police Officer of the City of Miami. Then I wanted to go to college, and I did! I attended "Miami Dade College School of Justice" and I was older than my classmates' parents and most of my professors, but this did not stop me. I had God with me.

I graduated from college with a BS Degree in Criminal Justice, graduating at the very top of my class, at the age of 56 as a straight-A student, and I was awarded "The Annual Outstanding Academic Achievement Award", which is given each year to the graduating student with the highest GPA! This award is the same as being chosen as the valedictorian in High School. Glory be to God!

All of this defies logic and medical science. Psychiatrists and psychologists suggest that my brain cells ought to have been destroyed or so badly damaged from decades of abuse that I should not have been able to graduate from college, much less graduate at the very top of my class as a straight-A student. Clearly, I could not have done it without God. Glory be to God!

I have become a righteous, respectable, responsible, successful, and productive member of society who is now 16 years sober, free, extremely happy, and full of joy. Glory be to God, Amen!

Before I turned my life over to the care of God, some people used to call me a piece of crap. Those people look at me now and call me "Mr. Lonnie". I do not have the right to remain silent, and I will shout it from the rooftops: I am a living witness to the absolute truth—that Jesus is still alive, and that He is still working in the lives of His people to this day, just as He did back in the day.

Author's Comments

Mr. Lonnie is indeed a living, walking, and talking miracle. I have never met him but was so thankful for his permission to share his story. The first thing that grabbed my heart was that Mr. Lonnie had a desire to live, and he knew that without God, he would not survive. He desperately sought God with his heart, mind, body, and soul. He came into God's presence with every stain, and beloved, when God says come as you are, he means just that. Bring your habits, bondage, lying spirits, absolutely everything! Come with it, he can make your life brand new, look at Mr. Lonnie. Transformed. God even kept his mind preserved through all the abuse of drugs and alcohol because he had a plan for my brother's life.

Isaiah 1:18 encourages us, "Come now, and let us reason together, saith the Lord. Though your sins are as scarlet, they shall be white as snow; though they are red like crimson, they shall be as wool." Mr. Lonnie did not lose hope and stopped praying when he did not receive the manifestation of what he prayed for the first day. He did not give up on the second day either. However, he persevered as he waited on God. (Isaiah 40:31 They that wait on the Lord God will renew their strength. He shall mount up with wings like an eagle, he shall run and not be weary, walk and not faint.)

When he was offered a dollar, he refused it. In James 4:7, the bible tells us to "submit yourselves therefore to God. Resist the devil and he will flee from you." Money can be a good thing, but when we use it to fund our bondages, it is a terrible thing. Only with God's wisdom could Mr. Lonnie have seen money to, on that specific day, be a terrible thing. That day, money represented the devil, and with a manifestation borne of a submission to God, Mr. Lonnie resisted that dollar. Brethren, we must submit to God fully and ask for his manifestation in our lives.

Chapter 4

THE ODDS OF ONE OUT OF A MILLION

God's Vessel: Sharon Blackmon

March 2016

AS I SAT IN THE DOCTORS' OFFICE STARING into space, I tried to figure out how in the world it got to that point. There I was, at 46 years old, I had lost one baby at 5 months—I had Joshua still-born—and lost two more babies, each between 6 and 8 weeks of pregnancy. It was most devastating losing Joshua because we bonded while he grew in my womb. I could feel him playing, kicking, and moving about. I had prayed for so long to have a baby, and God answered my prayer, but I couldn't understand why he allowed me to conceive, only to take him back from me, not once, but three times. Given the successive losses, the doctor stated that too much damage had been done to my womb, tubes, and ovaries, and so, it was over for me. My womb was filled with bleeding polyps, I bled all month, I was miserable. My body could not take anymore, and the emotional strain was getting the best of me. The doctor stated that the only way to solve the problem was to have a hysterectomy.

I realized that this was my best option. My situation was complicating everything in my life, and I had become anemic because of the blood loss. I was feeling weak all the time, losing sleep, and dealing with pain in the abdominal area on the regular. I decided that I had had enough; I could no longer continue the cycle. I consented to the procedure and told the doctor that since there is no other way, to start the process. After leaving the doctor's office, I was relieved, but not quite. I felt like a failure. I felt like my womanhood was being snatched away from me. I was not sure how this surgery would affect me, and I was afraid of feeling empty inside. But I knew it was best for me physically, mentally, and medically. The surgery was scheduled for the following month, April. So here I go.

April 2016

The surgery was scheduled for the 26th. I had to go and give blood and get instructions for aftercare and what to expect during and after the procedure. The doctor mentioned that it is a possibility that he can puncture my bowels because it is so close to where he will be performing the hysterectomy. However, he stated that I should not be concerned about that because the odds of that happening were one in a million. I gave him a side-eye, but I knew in whose hands my life ultimately rested in. No matter what, I was trusting God that all would be well.

This was the day of the surgery. I was so nervous; my insides were quivering. This was the first time I would be having a major surgery. I had to make sure that I did not put any lotion or deodorant on my body, and I was not fond of that at all. I do not like to be ashy or risk musk! But I understood the reasoning behind it all; better safe than sorry. I had to report to the hospital at 6:00am. I knew that I would be in the hospital for one day after surgery just to make sure that all was well, vital signs returned to normal, there was no fever, and that I could use the restroom. Thank God I did not go through this experience alone, my fiancé, James, was with me the entire ordeal.

After registering, we waited in the surgical waiting room until it was time for them to call me back into the room to get prepped for surgery. It was finally my turn to get prepped for surgery. The nurse guided us to a little room. There were no doors to the prep rooms, only pull-back curtains. I had to remove my clothes and put on the butt-out hospital gown. They asked me a series of questions and started the IV and placed the hospital band on my wrist. At this point, I started to shake. I was cold, but more nervous than anything. James was cool as a cucumber as usual. He was laughing and cracking jokes to try to keep my nerves down, and his. We had some wait time before going into the surgery room. We prayed and asked God to be with us in the room and to guide the doctors' hands. James held my hand and told me that everything would be all right.

It was finally time to be rolled out and into the surgery room. James kissed me on the forehead and off I went into surgery. All I could think about was, this is it. After today, no more babies. All my dreams and hopes of having children would be shattered. But I did look forward to having no cycles! No more bleeding, no more buying pads, no more pain. Now that I was happy about it, I arrived. They had a few more things to stick and poke in me and then it was time to put me to sleep. It is amazing how, one moment you are answering questions, and the next, you are out. The last time I looked at the clock, it was 8:30 am.

Groggy and barely able to wake up, I heard chattering. I could not get myself together. Fear came over me. I could barely move. My eyes kept opening and shutting. I tried to talk, but no sound came out. I tried to move but could not. I felt the nurse touch me and gently shake me. I heard her say "I need you to start breathing" and she was calling my name. I was trying to answer her. I thought my mouth was moving but apparently, it was not. Over and over, I heard them call my name. Finally, I was able to open my eyes. Everything was blurred. I was trying to focus. One of the nurses got in my face and called my name. I got a moan out and she just kept telling me to breathe. "Take deep breaths", she kept saying.

I finally came to my senses and realized that something was not right. I began to cry and shake. I muttered, "what's wrong?" I asked if something happened to me. I could see a little better. I looked up at the clock and it was 4:15 pm. I knew for certain then, that something was wrong. The nurses kept saying I need you to breathe. Jesus, I was darn near in panic mode. I asked for my fiancé. I was told they would keep him informed. Meanwhile, I did not know what had happened, but James did. After my surgery, I later learned he had been taken into the room where they give the dreadful news that someone has died. He said that he sat there in shock, and immediately called my mother. They would not tell him anything at first, so automatically, he was thinking the worst. I would have, too! My mom immediately went into prayer, alerted my siblings, and then started contacting others for prayer.

The doctor finally met James in the room and told him what had happened. The doctor had made a mistake and punctured my bowels. Yes, I was the "one out of a million" case that this happened to. They had to keep me open with clamps to hold my organs still and to keep my system from being poisoned from sepsis. They had to contact a

Gastroenterologist to come in and do emergency surgery on me to close the bowel. I laid for hours on the table. They were afraid that my system may have been poisoned because of how long I laid there, open. I did not know what had happened to me until later that night when James explained it all to me. I knew something else had taken place because of the way I was feeling. They were giving me the maximum amount of dosage that the law allowed to be administered to a patient. I was in ICU but did not realize it until a couple of days later. Because of the damage that took place during surgery, I could not have a bowel movement, and gas stayed trapped in my belly. The pains that were coming like waves in my stomach were almost unbearable. When the pain hit, I could hardly breathe. Although I was given medication to help me go and to help with the trapped gas, they did not work for me at all.

I laid there in pain and prayed for relief and release. It was not long before they got me up to start walking. Oh my! I was not ready, but I did it. I had not yet wrapped my mind around what had just happened to me. If it had not been for the Lord that was on my side, I would not be here today to share this testimony. I certainly could have gone another way. I realized that if sepsis had spilled into my system, I would have been dead in three days! All my organs would have turned into mush and just like that, my life would have been over. Jesus is truly a GREAT PHYSICIAN! Prayer works! No matter what you are faced with, even in death, God is with us, and He promises to never leave or forsake us. Today, I am alive, and I am so grateful for the hands of God that are upon my life.

Author's Comments

Praise Jesus! The odds of the doctor puncturing Sharon's bowels during surgery was one in a million! However, even with these odds, she and James did not take the surgery lightly, they called upon the Giver of Life. The key thing that blessed me the most about Sharon is that although she had suffered tremendous losses losing her babies, it was apparent that she never lost faith, or denied the sovereignty of God. Sharon stated that no matter what, she was trusting God. She made a declaration of faith even before being rolled back into surgery. Sharon and her husband James prayed together. The Bible, in Matthew 18:19, says that "if two or more touch and agree, asking anything in my name, I will do it". Sharon and James asked for specific things. They asked for God's presence in the room, and for God to guide the hands of the surgeons, and the outcome was simply miraculous! Even with her being open for as long as she was, she did not get poisoned!

James was a man of faith. He proclaimed that everything would be okay because faith is the substance of things we hope for, the evidence of things unseen (Hebrews 11:1). James could not see the outcome with his physical eyes, but with his spiritual eyes, he counted it done. Father Abraham was counted as righteous because he believed God.

Above all, God pulled Sharon back from the brink of death. The surgery could have easily gone sideways, but God's invoked presence in the surgery room kept Sharon alive. Hallelujah! May the Lord's presence always be with us.

Chapter 5

TWELVE YEARS LATER

God's Vessel: Shanesia Johnson

I ONCE WENT THROUGH SUCH A TIGHT financial situation that I could not fathom how I was going to get out of. I just could not see how. But I said, "God, I know if you told me to do it, you will provide the necessary resources."

There was a project that I had been longing to do, but I did not have the finances required, so I shelved it in the back of my mind. Twelve years later, God said, "DO IT," but first, He told me to sow a financial seed of $1,000 into a ministry. Now at that time, that amount was huge, but I was obedient, and I sowed that seed. From the day I did so, God showed me who He is, and the power that He carries. He made provisions for me to get everything that I needed, and I did not lack a thing. Looking back at that situation, it had seemed impossible at the time, but the bible says, "I will give you favor with man", and He did! I had people helping me get things off the ground without any hesitation, and at no cost! Look at God! Once I received the message, I chose to trust Him without doubt or fear, and I sowed the seed. I believe that when you need God to do something big in your life, it is important to give 'big'. The bible says, "Give, and it will be given to you. A good measure, pressed down, shaken together, and running over, will be poured into your lap. For with the measure you use, it all will be measured to you." Yes, it was financially tight, at times, painfully so, and looking back, I only made it happen by the grace of God. Week after week, He made a way for me, and he always came on time.

Just in the Knick of Time – Shanesia Johnson

Another testimony of God being just on time is that of one morning when my fiancé and I were in his car. My car was parked about 4 feet in front of his, and since it was during the cold months, he got out to warm my car up for me. When he stepped out, he forgot to put the car in park, and my first thought was, "OH MY GOD!"I was sure his car was going to bump into mine. My stepdaughter, Asiah, was in the back seat, and she said, "The car is rolling!" I jumped out and screamed, "Baaaaae, the car is rolling!" By then he was already in my car, busy turning on the heater, but he heard me and ran back and pressed his foot on the brake. His car stopped two inches from hitting my car. At that very moment, I felt God say, "Don't you ever doubt me. I am never early, never late!" He let me know that He will always provide for me in the nick of time!

Happy update: I did complete my original project! In my mind, it was nobody but God! Trust Him, wholeheartedly, and He will answer you.

Author's Comments

This is a beautiful story on why it is so important to wait on the Lord. Twelve years! That is how long it took. That is enough time for her to lose faith, enough time for her to "move on". But God answered her prayer because according to his word in Isaiah 40:31, "...they who wait for the Lord shall mount up with wings like eagles, they shall run and not be weary, they shall walk and not faint." Thank you, Lord!

One thing I know about this woman of God, Shanesia, is that she is a giver. I have never met her in person, but she has sown seeds on my behalf in others just because I asked. I have seen countless events that this woman of God has blessed and sowed in the lives of other vendors. I hope somebody catches this in the spirit. The law of sowing and reaping applies to everything. A hand that opens to receive, but never gives will never prosper. Shanesia was obedient to God when he told her to sow a financial seed that was a stretch for her at the time. She understood that to fear God was to trust him, so, she trusted him with her whole heart. One thing that tells me she trusted with her whole heart was not necessarily her words, it was her actions. That she sowed that seed despite being in need speaks volumes. She continues to give God credit that He did it. I believe it is important to give God the glory that is due to Him; it all belongs to Him because we cannot do anything without Him.

Chapter 6

FED UP

God's Vessel: Nicole Howard

I JUST WANT TO ENCOURAGE ANY YOUNG man or woman who is enduring any form of domestic abuse: physical, mental, or verbal. Here is my story:

For six long years, I suffered domestic violence of all forms. I was beaten, mentally abused, and the worst, verbally abused. I thought I would never get out of that situation. Every time I thought I was strong enough to leave, he would tell me that I would never be able to make it without him. I believed him. I endured so much pain and misery in those six years that I went into a deep depression. I started to believe that I was not worthy of love, that if I just did whatever he wanted, he would love me. How untrue, it only got worse, and he never loved me.

But GOD...on June 1, I prayed. Even though I had prayed before, that time was different. This prayer came from my inner man, straight from the heart. On this day, I was so fed up that there was no way I could take another day of abuse. I wanted him gone from my life! So, that night, I lay in my bed and I prayed to our Heavenly Father, I prayed so long and so hard that I fell asleep. The very next day when I awoke, I felt so free and so liberated, and to my relief, he had finally packed his things and left. The moral of the story is that GOD may not come when you want him but he is always on time.

Author's Comments

How often we hear about the devastating impacts of physical and mental abuse on its survivors; not everyone makes it out alive or in one piece. I am so sincerely thankful that our sister in Christ and my former classmate, Nicole, was not another statistic. Although she endured this abuse for a long time, she made the best decision that possibly saved her life. How often do we hear the story of the man or woman that could not just leave? Be it out of fear, the kids, or some other reason, and choosing to stay cost them a limb or their lives. It could be any of us, or anyone in our circle of friends and family. Like Nicole, prayer is always a wonderful step to get anyone out of these situations. The key things that I believe every reader should take away from Nicole's testimony is as follows:

1. She prayed to God for strength. Beloved, any time you attempt to leave a situation like this, but find yourself being convinced to stay and try one more time, and that one more time becomes a repeated cycle, you have to look to God to be your strength. (2 Corinthians 12:10: "Yes, I am glad to be weak or insulted or mistreated or to have troubles and sufferings if it is for Christ. Because when I am weak, I am strong"). Friends never be ashamed when you find

yourself in situations like this and shame could be what cost the most valuable thing that can never be replaced. Your life!

2. Pray with fervor. Nicole had been praying, but one day, it was no longer just the regular prayer. Even Jesus frequently prayed fervently; although he often prayed, many times, he was described as having prayed "fervently". This goes to prove that there is a kind of prayer where you give of yourself so much that God is moved to you. Here, we see Nicole fervently pray herself into freedom. Beloved, how do you pray? How fervently do you pray? Do you make the time to pray fervently or do you always pray on the go? Do not get me wrong, praying on the go is excellent, but do you make special time to pray fervently? We all should; you should.

Chapter 7

THAT IS ENOUGH

God's Vessel: James McCluney

MY NAME IS JAMES MCCLUNEY. I WAS born and raised in Gaffney, SC. My mother was young when she birthed me, so my grandparents raised me. It was a hard life of farming and crop sharing to survive. I was raised with my aunts, uncle, and cousins, and, being the oldest grandson, we varied in age from 3 to 12 years apart. My grandfather was an alcoholic, a womanizer, and abuser, and kept our household walking on eggshells. He was in and out of jail, and on the chain gang pretty much my entire childhood. My grandmother would take us to church when she could get a ride, which was not often. Growing up, I did not see either of my parents on birthdays or Christmas much. My aunts left home after high school, uncle went to Vietnam, and cousins went back to live with their dad. I had sworn to myself not to become an alcoholic like my grandfather. In my teenage years, nothing much changed at home, and I became increasingly embarrassed when friends came over. Between the ages of 15 and 17, I intentionally buried myself in sports just to be away from home.

I was introduced to marijuana at a basketball game in the 12th grade. I had heard about marijuana, but I did not have any knowledge of it. I turned it down several times until one night, during halftime at a basketball game. On taking it, I played the game of my life that night, or so I thought at the time, but what I did not know was that marijuana would become my gateway drug.

When I turned 17, I convinced my mom to take me down to the recruiting center to sign up for the military, not knowing what I was doing. I just wanted to get away from home. I joined the military, and, while stationed in San Antonio, Texas, I tried marijuana again and again. When I left Texas, I went to Kansas and continued my marijuana use, and this time, being stationed with a hospital unit, drugs were easily accessible. My use of marijuana opened me up to try harder drugs like acid, snorting cocaine, and crack. Exercising daily made me feel like I was performing at a high level. I was in the Army for 6 years. My mindset was to "work hard, play hard", so I partied like my life depended on it.

I left the military and did not change anything for the betterment of my life. I continued partying, and, according to the world's standard, I was doing great—I had multiple bank accounts with at least four digits and a well-paying job, and I purchased my first home at the age of 27. During this time, partying was happening all weekend, and while partying, I was introduced to crack-cocaine.

Within the first year of living in my home, I was laid off and things started to change. I lost my home and had to move back in with my grandparents. My grandmother was tickled to death to have me home again. My grandmother's health was failing, but I did not notice it because of my selfish drug life. One dreadful day after hanging out at a friend's house, I walked into the house and found my grandmother slumped over in her favorite chair. She had passed away. The thing I feared most had come to pass and I was mortified! My drug addiction became even worse after that incident. I left Gaffney, SC, and got a job driving 18 wheelers in a bid to escape from the drugs. It worked for a while until someone rear-ended me at speeds close to 100mph on I 40 East in Knoxville, Tennessee. I quit driving and resumed getting high. I did a range of crazy stuff that led to jail time for 6 misdemeanors. The judge gave me 90 days in SCDC, which was unusual for first-time offenders. I spent 10 days in Perry's prison for processing, and on the 8th day, the prison minister came through, and I accepted Jesus Christ as my personal Savior. When I went to my next destination, I was favored the entire time I was in the system. I was given administrative-type jobs. God favored me. I did 82 days and was released here in

Greenville, SC. It seemed like people were willing to help me succeed. My counselor at the pre-release center suggested going to the Greenville Rescue Mission to get a new start in life, and I had no idea what to expect. After being at the Mission, I signed up for trade school to be an electrician helper, a course which took 12 weeks. After finishing school, we were hired by Fluor for a project in LaGrange, GA that would last up to a year. As a new believer, I had no plans for being fed spiritually. I was working 7 days a week, 12 hours a day. After 3 months at work, I found myself going back to some of my old habits, chasing girls, and smoking crack. This behavior continued for about 3 months until one morning, around 4am, I was sitting at a table full of crack and I heard a voice say, "that's enough". After smoking crack all night and into the morning, when I heard that voice, I stood up and emptied my pockets of everything. I had people asking where I was going, and I said, "I don't know". I left to get dressed for work and while putting my boots on, I realized blood was leaking from my nose. Then I fell on my knees and asked God to forgive me and restore my mind and heart. While at work that day, I met a special woman with the presence of God all over her, and I got a conviction in my spirit to do what needed to be done. I turned my badge in and my supervisor offered me more money to stay. I said that I had to take care of something first. I took the Greyhound back to Greenville and checked back into the Greenville Rescue Mission. The Mission had a Christ-centered alcohol and drug program that lasted 3 months. After the program, I expressed interest in going to Bible College, and they said I had to wait a year to make sure I was still clean. The year flew by and I was accepted into Holmes Bible College. I was voted as a freshman class president. God favored me in so many ways. I attended there for 2 years, sharing my testimony, and doing company fundraising. I was subsequently given a job as a night supervisor at the Greenville Rescue Mission. I was quickly sought out to do commercials for Miracle Hill and as the single ministry speaker from Tennessee to Charleston. It seemed like God was moving me quickly in front of prestigious people. I was attending North Hills Community Church and they poured into my life big time, from cars to tuition. I was speaking and sharing my testimony in big local churches. I shared my testimony with the prison I had previously served time in. After I left, I met my wife Alice at church in 1997. God was moving. We got married in 2000 and God blessed us with a son, and we named him Isaiah. Today, I am retired, and I work in my community as a mentor with Greenville county schools, and co-pastor in my hometown Gaffney. Our God is a sovereign God who is full of grace and mercy.

Author's Comments

Deliverance out of trouble is a form of God's mercy being enacted because of a covenant.

Look at the grace and mercy God showed James. I must admit that my first thought was that James had a praying grandmother. The prayers she said continued to work in James' life.

Friends, God is a covenant-keeping God as he said to us in Isaiah 59:21, "And as for me, this is my covenant with them…My spirit that is upon you, and my words that I have put in your mouth, shall not depart out of your mouth or out of the mouth of your offspring, or out of the mouth of your children's offspring…from this time forth and forevermore".

God always keeps his word. But you have got to listen AND obey. James heard the voice of the Lord saying, "that's enough" and he obeyed! This was the important step: listening and doing. Trust and obey, for the Lord has only plans to prosper you.

Even when the enemy got a hold of James again, he prayed and cried out to God for deliverance and restoration. And God came through like he always does, in the person of the special woman James met. The devil came again in the form of more money to keep him in his position, to keep him away from God's calling. But James, convinced of God's message, turned down money to go to rehab, went to bible college and became a living testimony to others about another snare of the devil – addiction.

Although James did not want to become an alcoholic like his grandfather, the enemy got him addicted to something else, something worse. Yet he overcame the enemy asking, listening, trusting, and obeying. Glory to God!

Chapter 8

UNSHACKLED BY THE DEPRESSION CURER

God's Vessel: Benita Lawrence

MY NAME IS BENITA LAWRENCE. I HAVE been a minister of the gospel for over 20 years, and I know how it feels to be depressed and immersed in a feeling of emotional hopelessness. I had regular depressive bouts with negative thoughts and feelings of gloominess, although I was saved and filled with God's Spirit, and was preaching the gospel. There were times when I could not lift my head from the pillow on my bed because of the weight of negative emotions. I also suffered from paralyzing anxiety, intrusive thoughts, and symptoms of schizophrenia. Through a tumultuous journey, I have learned that we can be susceptible to depression through various doorways, but its ultimate source is the devil. Meditating on negative thoughts and embracing negative emotions became a part of my daily life. I began to experience a sick satisfaction during times of isolation as I sunk deeper into a pit of self-absorption. On the one hand, I liked it because it gave me justification for being disappointed with life and being angry with God. On the other hand, I hated being depressed because meditating on negativity never solved the problems that I was depressed about.

As time progressed and because there was no interruption, I felt like I was under a spell that had consumed me. I became addicted to being depressed, and unknowingly created a soul tie or emotional tie with the gloom. I felt completely hopeless and as a result, I attempted suicide repeatedly. I took an overdose of pills multiple times, cut my wrist, stabbed myself, attempted to starve myself, attempted to dehydrate myself, made arrangements for a gun purchase, left home in the middle of the night hoping to be killed, hitch-hiked with strangers, purchased rat poison and went to the river and contemplated jumping in. I even attempted to hire countless people to murder me. I have been handcuffed after running from the police, strapped down with restraints, been on 24-hour watch in the psychiatric ward, and given psychotropic drugs for depression.

I was diagnosed and medically treated for severe depression in addition to other mental disorders. I met with psychiatrists, counselors, social workers, and pastors. I went around and around in a circle of depression for years. Finally, I learned that I had to roll up my sleeves and go to work managing the thoughts and feelings that were within. I learned that God had given me authority over my soul, and I could say NO to depression. After a grueling battle with it, God revealed to me that depression, spiritually speaking, is a demonic attack on the human soul, which includes the mind, emotions and the human will, instead of a punishment from God or a sign of a lack of faith. I learned that anyone, even Christians, can struggle with depression.

I ultimately emerged from depression when I learned how to partner with His Spirit and not only come out but stay out of the grip of depression. God, who is the depression curer, has equipped me with insight and strategies to assist others in their journey to overcome it. As a result, I have authored books to help Depressed Believers, their family members, and ministerial staff, to learn how to effectively reach and minister to them.

I have been blessed to have a closed Facebook group called "Un-shackled From Depression" and a YouTube channel with the same name. In both the Facebook group and on the YouTube channel, there are revelatory teachings, poems, and songs that encourage those who are struggling with depression or desire to emerge from the claws of depression. My assignment concerning Depression in the Body of Christ is five-fold:

1. To demystify depression by providing a simplified, spiritually based definition.

2. To encourage believers to be unashamed about facing depression.
3. To encourage believers to fully embrace the ministry of the Holy Spirit, and to invite Him to partner with them as He reveals Himself as the Depression Curer.
4. To provide hope and strategies to emerge from depression and maintain a healthy soul by sharing my testimony and experiences.
5. To assist God's leaders to reach and effectively minister to those who are depressed.

God delivered me from my depressive state; He can deliver you from yours, too. In fact, he wants to. All you need do is open your heart and mind to him.

Author's Comments

I enjoyed the transparency in Mrs. Lawrence's testimony. It brought a fresh perspective and touches on a topic that many believers may not feel comfortable talking about depression. Mrs. Lawrence suffered grave depression, and her testimony is proof that depression is not of God, and that God can lift any sufferer out of it! Even better, what was a low point of her life became the basis for God's gift to the world through her. Amazing!

Meditating on negativity and embracing negative emotions is a trick the enemy uses to open portals to the spirit of depression. The word tells us in Romans 12:2 to "be not conformed to this world but be transformed by the renewal of your mind." Friends, it is extremely important to take every thought captive. God speaks to us through Philippians 4:8, saying, "whatever is noble, whatever is right, whatever is pure, whatever is lovely, whatever is admirable, if anything is excellent or praiseworthy, think on these things." Isn't it wonderful that there is a Bible verse for just any life situation?! He has given us the word to feed on, to nourish our souls, to meditate upon, to empower ourselves, and to have power and authority over the wiles of the devil. Beloved, you have been given every defense against the devil, use them, that all glory may be to His name.

Chapter 9

JEHOVAH RAPHA

God's Vessel: Tracey Moss

I GIVE ALL PRAISE, HONOR, AND GLORY TO the Highest God for all he has done in my life. The enemy has been relentless in his attacks against me. I have suffered from paralysis and blindness from flares of Multiple Sclerosis. Friends, Jehovah Rapha intervened and performed a mighty miracle and healed my body. Even during the times of paralysis, He was there. He was my eyes when I could not see, my legs when I could not walk. I am so thankful that the suffering that I have endured is not apparent in my physical walk. Psalm 91:4 says, "He shall cover thee with his feathers, and under his wings shalt thou trust, His truth shall be thy shield and buckler." As for God, His ways are perfect. The word of the Lord is flawless. Saints, the enemy will continue to be relentless in his attempts to destroy God's children. Even after the mighty miracle of healing from blindness and paralysis, the enemy attacked my mind, I became severely depressed, I lost my memory, and he even tried to steal my sanity. But for God! Isaiah 59:19 says, "when the enemy comes in like a flood, the spirit of God will raise a standard against him." That is exactly what He did for me. Jeremiah 30:17 declared that "…I will restore you to health and heal your wounds". Today I am the proud owner of 3 homes, 3 cars, a reputable business, and more. Saints, I encourage you to keep the faith. Storms and trials will come, sickness will come but there is nothing too hard for God. He can and will do just what he said.

Author's Comments

Unbelievable! Praise God! My jaw dropped as I read that but of course, there is nothing too much for God; our minds are simply too small to comprehend just how marvelous and omnipotent He is. Restored from paralysis and blindness! What a miracle! This is just as God promised in Joel 2:25 that He will "restore to you the years that the locust hath eaten, the cankerworm, and the caterpillar, and the palmerworm, my great army which I sent among you" (KJV). And even then, the enemy came back, trying to steal more, but Tracey was firmly in God's hands.

Tracey had a role to play in all of this. She recognized the sovereignty of God and trusted Him with all she had. She recognized that her afflictions were merely different forms of temptations, and even while paralyzed and blind, she never gave up, instead, she continued to bless the name of the Lord. Her steadfastness in the Lord and His promises was simply unwavering!

Today, she is encouraging us and reminding us that afflictions and trials will come, but none of them are too big for God to handle. She was relentless in her faith and God showed up for her. If He did it for her, He will do it for you because He hearkens to those who call on His name.

Chapter 10

MY PAST DOES NOT DEFINE ME

God's Vessel: Ava Banks

GOD TOLD ME THAT THIS YEAR, I NEEDED to start sharing my story more, so here goes.

I had never really shared my testimony in detail because I had still been battling with most of the demons that kept me up at night. I was deeply ashamed to touch on the depths of where God had brought me from! I was afraid of what man would think, and of the judgment that would follow, until I realized that the only judgment that I should fear was that which came from God, the very God that brought me out to show others that he could indeed do the same for anyone else, and could use anyone else that was simply willing to give him their Yes!

I grew up being molested in my mother's home by a friend of hers starting at the age of 6 until the age of 12. I remember nights of him sneaking and standing over my bed, silently forcing his way in. My mother KNOWINGLY turned a blind eye. I grew up without a father and watched as my mother jumped from man to man and suffered abuse from almost every one of them that crossed our path! I used to watch my alcoholic stepfather attempt to beat my mother to death nearly every night. Sometimes, he turned his rage toward me; I remember once being locked in our fridge for what often felt like hours. I remember us having to leave often with nowhere to go and sleeping in the streets. It was hard, listening to my mother explain why we were sleeping in a car. By the 3rd grade, I started to experience abuse at my mother's hands. I was told that I would not amount to anything in life, that I was better off dead, that she hoped a car would kill me out in the streets. I remember being stabbed in the knees, unable to walk, having my head slammed against the walls on almost a daily basis, and having bonnet pepper be smeared into my eyes. The frequent threats to kill me if I ever told anyone of the abuse made me suffer silently. Along with everything I faced at home, I began to get bullied at school. Still, I suffered silently, believing that no one would care! I always wore a smile to mask the pain.

I became depressed and started to attempt suicide, never really having the guts to go through with it at any point. By 13, I started running away from home and looking for love in all the wrong places. I started to cut up my arms as a form of outlet by middle school. By 16, I had been admitted into the mental hospital 3 times for suicide attempts. I became homeless at the age of 16, moving from place to place. I was beaten and raped, I slept at bus stops and in abandoned houses. Still, through it all, I smiled.

At 16, I finally met my birth father for the very first time, but shortly after, he tried to kill me. Following that, I grew to have no sense of value for life, I struggled with low self-esteem, I hated myself, I hated life, I hated God for creating me and allowing me to suffer the way that I did! I started smoking to ease the pain, nothing worked. I was alone, out on the streets, with nowhere to go! I had no legal documents (my green card & social security card had been stolen) and I could not get a job. My life was taking wrong turn after wrong turn. Survival mode became my norm so eventually, I ended up dancing, although I was self-conscious and hated my body. Liquor gave me the courage that I needed to get through the nights. I met an older man who sold false dreams to me, talked about how he could give me a better life and how I would not want for anything. As a naive, broken girl, I believed him! I started being trafficked, believing that if I just did what I was told, that it'd make him happy, which in turn, would probably lead to me being happy, and hopefully, having a better life. I was dying on the inside and silently crying out for help! I remember being in middle and high school and reaching out for help, but no one batted an eyelid. My daily reality was simply being brushed to the side, and sometimes, I felt invisible. I was made out to be a liar, so, no matter how much I was begging to die inside, leave it to me, I was always okay! But who would have known that I was the girl that no matter how many blows life had thrown my way, kept a fake smile plastered on my face and a false sense of joy? I became a mule, and everything was yes, with a smile, no matter how painful it truly was. I became exposed to a world that I had previously known only on television. Nothing glamorous of course, but simply the dark side of music execs, penthouses, crack-cocaine, and lustful desires. I soon ended up in the industry. Life had taken its toll! There I was, at the tender age of 18, and had already experienced so many things that people could not even come to imagine! I remember being in my room at 18 one afternoon, ready to dance with death again!

You see, like many people, I grew up in church, but I did not know God! I did not have a relationship with Jesus! Come to think of it, I did not even believe in Jesus! That afternoon, I remember crying out to God! I did not know how to pray. I just screamed and shouted, expressing every bit of pain I felt in my soul! I cried and begged him to call me home! I was tired of the voices in my head that were often louder than my thoughts! I was tired of the depression, of feeling, and being worthless! I was tired of having no one! I decided again that I would attempt to take my life! I remember crying in my room, with a bottle of pills in my hands. A handful at a time, I was shoving them down my throat! I remember it as if it were yesterday, hearing God speak! The voice said, "You're not going to die, you're wasting your time because I have plans for you!" I remember surrendering it all to God! Giving him everything! I remember being in the hospital room afterward, unharmed and with no internal damage done, even after overdosing on painkillers! There was this super bright light in the room. There, in the light, seemed to be a figure. After that day, my life has never been the same! A few months later, I was invited to a church, Worldwide Kingdom Ministries, and I gave my life to Christ. God delivered me from depression, from suicidal thoughts, from so many things that I cannot even name! In 2013, at the age of 18, the old me died, and God began to change me from the inside out! He showed me his love and his purpose for my life! He took someone like me that everyone had discarded, someone that was broken, and He washed me clean and began to use me. He showed me that the fact that no one saw my value did not mean that I was worthless!!!!

Today, I share my story to say that no matter how far gone, or how far damaged you are, God has a plan for your life! God can use you, transforming you, and putting every broken piece back together! Everyone he used in the Bible had an issue, had a past, and according to man, should not have been worthy! But God used them anyway! Because God does not call the qualified, He qualifies the call, and all he needs is a YES!

There is FREEDOM in Jesus! I feel it today and have felt it since that day when I was 18. There is NOTHING too impossible or too hard for him to do! Just look at where he brought me from. Just give him your YES! I do not share my Testimony for pity, BUT TO GIVE GOD THE GLORY!

Author's Comments

Ava's story is a truly heart-wrenching and motivating one. She has been through it all – physically abused, mentally abused, sexually abused, all by people with whom she was supposed to be safe. It did not stop there, she battled depression, drugs, sexual depravity, and nearly died. But none of this matter because all along, God had a plan for her. Her telling this testimony is a part of that plan; I feel truly humbled and blessed at how God works, and how He hears and shows up for his people.

Ava never felt love for a day in her life, not at home, not at school, so she sought love in the wrong places. But she did not find it. But when she found God, or rather, when she said yes to God, God's overflowing love enveloped her and transformed her life.

Saints, I want you to understand that no matter how bad life gets, there is always light at the end of the tunnel, as was the case with Ava. She came clean with herself and realized that despite having heard about God throughout her childhood, she never quite had a close personal relationship with Him, and she sought that relationship, by all means, calling on His name and seeking His face. He, in turn, heard her cries and revealed himself to her. What an amazing God! God always saves His people, brethren. He heals them, He cleanses them of their sins, cleanses their minds, and makes them whole again. We, as humans may feel unworthy sometimes, we may feel dirty, used, and unclean, but God ALWAYS calls the unfit and makes them fit for His personal use. Ava heard and recognized the voice of God. She knew that by calling on His name, her problems would be over, and she obeyed when God spoke to her. Praise be unto His name for her salvation!

Chapter 11

FOR WHO THE SON SETS FREE IS FREE INDEED

God's Vessel: Andre Miles

PART 1

I HAVE BEEN SET FREE FROM MASTURBA-tion, stealing from stores (my excuse being that they are too expensive), fornicating with prostitutes, etc. I have been set free from lying, pornography, adultery, profanity, having a wicked tongue, and speaking curses over people. I am free from witchcraft (the spirit of stubbornness), and mental illness – I went to the psych ward 11 times in 5 years. I am free from idolatry, sun worship, worshipping women, orgies, and many more that I do not remember now. Please share my testimony, for we are overcome by the blood of the Lamb and the word of our testimonies.

PART 2

I always believed in God, but not his only begotten son Jesus Christ. I did not grow up in the church, but I attended a few churches growing up.

From May 5th, 2013, I was remanded in a mental ward 11 times within 5 years and experienced so much from Satan and his demons on this earth. I took over 15 different medicines and none worked – they only polluted and toxified my temple. When I was on Seroquel at the hospital, I heard from within that I am under hypnosis. But Satan is a liar and does not have power over God's own.

PART 3

I remember years ago, I was fasting, and I started tooting my horn because I was fasting and made a video. I watched my video after and noticed my head went down real fast and came back up real fast. Then I was led to Isaiah 58 (KJV) and I automatically glanced at verse 5 and it shocked me. It says, "Is it such a fast that I have chosen? A day for a man to afflict his soul? Is it to bow down his head like a bulrush? ..." This was exactly what I did in the video! God must have forced my head to go down so fast. After reading that, I immediately got scared and repented and deleted my video in shock.

When I was in the psych ward, through the Holy Spirit, I prayed for a man in a wheelchair who had trouble walking and was having daily or weekly seizures. After I prayed for him, the next day, he started walking and while I was there, he was not having any seizures. He was also a believer in Jesus. All praise be to Him.

Another time, I was in the psych ward as a baby in Christ in 2014, a year after my conversion, and I prayed for two ladies in a circle holding hands, and one lady said she felt 5 demons leave her body – the spirit of anxiety, depression, and others that I have forgotten.

All I can say from these experiences is that God and Jesus are the only way to eternal life. Matthew 7:13-14 reminds us that wide is the gate and broad is the road that leads to destruction, and many enter through it.

Zephaniah 2:1-3 says, "Gather together, yes, gather, o shameless nation, before the decree takes effect before the day passes away like chaff before there comes upon you the burning anger of the Lord, before there comes upon you the day of the anger of the Lord. Seek the Lord, all you humble of the land, who do His just commands; seek righteousness; seek humility; perhaps you may be hidden on the day of the anger of the Lord."

Author's Comments

This is incredible! God is alive indeed! Saved from 5 years of being remanded in an institution and being fed chemicals that were only toxifying Andre's body. Saved from the sins of the flesh. Saved, and through the power of the Holy Spirit, secured the healing of another. Praise Jesus! Saints, God's will is perfect. Who would have thought that a thieving, lustful, lying, adulterous, wicked, hateful, and mentally ill person could become God's very own vessel? Man would have condemned him! But not our God, because His will is perfect, and His timing is perfect.

Andre was on the broad road; he was of the world. Even after he became saved, he kept following the trends of the world, making videos of himself fasting. But God saved him from himself. He found the narrow way, the only way that leads to eternal life, the way that only a few will find. Indeed, many are called but a few are chosen, but God called Andre and chose him. May His name be praised!

Chapter 12

30 YEARS OF TURMOIL; 50 YEARS OF TRUST

God's Vessel: Jerome Cofield

YOUR LIFE HAS A PURPOSE. EVEN WHEN you cannot trace God, trust Him. When you cannot understand what is going on, trust Him. Just trust Him. It can be difficult, but just do it. I hope my story inspires you.

I was born on 31st July 1966.

In 1974, my daddy left me, and I found myself hurting and just wanting my daddy.

In 1975, my parents' divorce was finalized. I was officially living in a single-parent home.

From 1975-1984, I was told thousands of times, "You will never be anything".

In 1984, I graduated high school.

In 1986, I suffered a stroke that left me paralyzed on the left side of my body.

In 1987, I did not understand why Regina R. Woodgett would step into this world of chaos to become Mrs. Cofield (my wife).

In 1988, in the middle of rehab, I suffered a stroke for the second time, which paralyzed the left side of my body again.

In 1991, I was diagnosed with Guillain-Barre Transverse Myelitis, which left me paralyzed in both legs and left arm, partially paralyzed in the right arm, and my vocal cords were 100% paralyzed. My wife was told by four different doctors at three different hospitals that, "this is it, his life is over". But by this time, it was making sense why she came into my life four years earlier because when I couldn't declare it for myself, she would declare it for me: "He will live and not die".

In 1992, I was still hanging in there, but was told I might want to go on disability as nobody would ever hire me because of my preexisting condition; that I would be a liability to anybody's company.

In 1999, I found myself walking alongside a dirt road picking up aluminum cans to sell, so that I would feel like a man, husband, and father, contributing to the house.

In 2000, I started writing a vision of what I wanted for myself. I wrote that if I ever went back to work again, this is what I would do: bless as many people as possible. Not only was I writing a vision, I started to change my way of thinking, and began to dream and think BIG.

In 2006, I became the CEO of the non-profit organization "Make a Child Smile Foundation Inc." of Georgia.

In 2015, I was approached, approved of, and hired by Ms. Debra Brock, principal at Whitesville Road Elementary School, after being told twenty years earlier that nobody would hire me.

In 2016, at age 50, my life shifted, and Romans 8:31 came into view; "What shall we then say to these things? If God is for us, who can be against us?" Also, 1 Corinthians 2:9 which says, "But as it is written, eye hath not seen, nor ear heard, neither have entered into the heart of man, the things which God hath prepared for them that love him." These two passages of scripture became life for me.

Thirty years of turmoil. I told my story just to say to you: although you may feel cut down or cut off from the one who created you, the one that is known as the Life-Giver, you can always start over, yes, even at 50 years old. He can always give you a fresh start.

Author's Comments

30 years of strife and sorrow. 30 years living through being abandoned by a father, being told you would not amount to anything, suffering multiple strokes, suffering multiple paralysis, being written off as "no-good", being asked to go on disability because no one would hire you. Most people would have lost faith, descended into all sorts of sin – alcoholism, abuse, negativity, etc. But Jerome knew and trusted God. He trusted God with everything he had. Even with multiple strokes, he trusted God. Through multiple paralysis, he trusted God. God sent him an Angel, his wife, to speak life into him when he was not able to. God kept him.

It should also be noted that his missing rib came into his life just in the nick of time. God placed Regina Woodgett in Jerome's life for a reason and she, in turn, fulfilled God's wishes. She loved, believed, and trusted in God with all her heart and uplifted and prayed for her husband. Her will and determination to speak life into him are extremely admirable and speak volumes of their unwavering trust in God. She could have easily walked away, but she knew that God always has a perfect plan, because she was a part of that perfect plan for Jerome's life.

It is important, brethren, that we become partners with people whose interests, beliefs, and values mirror ours, so we do not find ourselves at sea when life's trials come knocking. More importantly, seek God's face in choosing your partner. Get God's confirmation on your relationship, and I promise you, that relationship will only propel you toward your destined future. He is already in your future, for He planned it himself. Trust Him always, for He is the same God yesterday, today, and forevermore. Amen.

Chapter 13

GOD IS NEVER LATE

God's Vessel: Alice Garner

MY NAME IS ALICE GARNER AND I AM CUR-rently married with 8 children. We are a blended family, with my husband and I originally entering the union with four children each.

I was born and raised in Georgia, and growing up, my family did not have much. There were 6 of us living in a 2-room shack—2 adults and 4 kids—with no hydro or bathroom facilities. Despite their best efforts, our parents eked out a meager living as we youngsters worked every day in pine straw. We still barely had food at times, and second-hand clothes were the norm. Sometimes, the clothes were given to us, and other times, we found them in trash cans. In high school, my family was finally able to get a used trailer that had more rooms for us, but we still did not have running water. I started working at KFC when I turned 16 so that I could help with the financial needs of my family after my brother died in 2003. I graduated in 2004, while pregnant with my first child. When I got married in 2005, I was still trying to help my parents and take care of my new family, so we were struggling.

Our first year of marriage was decent, but my then husband was not working much, and, by the time we had two children, he had begun to stray. By 2007, after he had moved out a couple of times, I had to move back home with my 2 children because I could no longer afford to live in my apartment without help. By the end of 2007, I was able to get back on my feet enough to find a place for us to stay, and my estranged husband moved back in. The beginning of 2008 started roughly again, with my husband doing the same things as before, and by June, I had joined the Military. The day before I graduated basic training, I found out that my spouse had fathered a child with someone else. Using every effort to keep my family together, I ended up moving to Arizona with my family at the end of that same year. Unsurprisingly, things remained the same. After being deployed to Afghanistan in 2012, I found out that my husband was back to his cheating ways and had fathered another child. I finally got up enough courage to leave him, once and for all, upon returning from Afghanistan. He responded to this news by pulling a gun on me and told me I was not going anywhere. That was a terrifying time, to say the least. Soon (April 2013), it was time for me to move to my next duty station, so I convinced him to stay in Arizona, assuring him that I would return after my tour, and get out of the Army. After leaving Arizona, I never looked back, and I filed for a divorce that was granted in 2014. Sadly, I ended up falling for the same traits in someone else, which also ended up in heart-break. Moving onward and upward with my children, I prayed and prayed that God would send me someone who would treat us lovingly, but I had become cold-hearted, and could barely hope.

In 2016, the Army moved me to Japan, and I was still a single woman with four kids, in a foreign country. I ended up running into an old acquaintance who was also in the Army, and we became friends. He helped me with the kids, and although our friendship started to turn into a little more, I honestly was not ready because I still had not dealt with the hurt and pain that was inside of me. My pain caused me to sabotage our relationship, but he persisted. Although he was relocated from Japan, we remained together. Even when we were having problems, he was still there for the kids. I ended up getting diagnosed with the early stages of cervical cancer and, due to surgical complications, I was sent back to the States for treatment. I was blessed to have been sent to the same place where he was stationed. Our initial house purchase fell through, and I ended up getting medically retired from the Army. I started going to church, but still had not dealt much with my past or what it all meant. One

Sunday, I received a word from God to release the hurt and pain and give it to Him. Later that day, everything started changing as soon as I was able to do as God said. My partner began attending church with me, and we decided to get married and make things right with God and ourselves. After trusting and believing in God, everything started to come together. After the rejection of the previous year, we felt blessed to be approved for the purchase of a 4600 sq. ft house. God placed us together at a time when we needed each other. It does not matter where you came from, or what you have been through, God has ordained your plan. It is all going to work out in His timing, and all you need is faith and belief in the process. He will never leave nor forsake you!

Author's Comments

What an inspiring read! Alice went from living in a trailer with barely any space to owning a 4,600 sq. ft home! Went from not having water or bathroom facilities to having it all, went from struggling to make ends meet to working in the Army, went from an abusive, adulterous marriage and bad relationships to a loving, faithful marriage, and most importantly, went from a Godless marriage to a Godly one! Praise Jesus!

Alice had had too many struggles in life, so she had not realized how much hurt and pain she held on to. But when she received a word from God, telling her to let go of all her pain, to unburden her problems unto Him, she listened and obeyed. She understood that God's plans for us are for the best. And because she trusted, God sent her a loving partner, who loved her for who she was, and was willing to follow her to the House of God to make things right between them, and in the presence of God. They both trusted and believed fervently in God, believing that things would work out for them, and it did!

Saints, do you trust God's plan for your life? Do you listen to the voice of God? Do you obey the instructions that God put in your heart? I sincerely hope that we all come to a place where we can listen and obey God and his instructions because He knows better than us what we need, what is good for us. He has carved our futures and hand-picked our partners. All you need to do is meditate on His word, listen, and obey, and his promises for your life will come to pass. Amen.

Chapter 14

MY BURDENS ARE HIS

God's Vessel: Joyce Dunson

I HAD A STROKE IN 2008, FOR THE FIRST time. Early on a Thursday morning when I was to start a new job, I got up and prepared breakfast for my husband and me. I had taken some sea salt to clean out my system, then we sat down to eat. After eating, I got up and went to the sink and while doing the dishes, a cup slipped from my hand, and I fell to the floor, right beside the trash can. My husband asked what was wrong and I said I did not know. He said I was having a stroke, and then called for help. The ambulance came, and when they checked me out, my blood pressure was 250/150, so they had to airlift me to Emory Hospital. I was admitted into the ICU, where I stayed for 4 days, then was moved to the Rehabilitation Center for 3 weeks. After I got out of the hospital, I had to go to Rehab every other day for about 2 months. Bills started to come in the mail. I had no kind of insurance at all. I started praying to God, holding the bill up to Him, saying "You knew that this was going to happen and that I don't have any way to pay it". Then the bill for me being airlifted to the hospital came and it was $12,000. I had no way to pay it, so I gave that to God as well. The total of all the bills was way over $100,000. I gave them all to God and prayed and thanked Him for paying them and I believed that the bills were paid. One day, when I got the mail, I got what I thought was a bill and I was going to put it in file 13 (the trash) but the Spirit of God said to read it, so I did, and it read, "All your bills have been paid in full." I started to shout, thanking God, praising Him, and, despite the brace on my left leg, tried to dance – I was too overjoyed not to. So, YES! God can and will pay off any bill. PRAISE BE TO GOD!!

Author's Comments

Joyce's experience of God is truly phenomenal. From having a stroke and having no means of paying her hospital bills to having all her bills paid in full! This is amazing! But it is also to be expected; Matthew 11:28 (KJV) says, "Come unto me, all ye that labor and are heavily laden, and I will give you rest." Joyce followed this exact portion of the Bible, casting her woes, her bills, and problems unto the Almighty, even when she did not know how He would do it, and she was given rest. He turned around what looked like a hopeless situation in her favor. God has never failed those who believe in His name and He will never.

Saints, what is that burden you carry? What is that burden that seems insurmountable? What is that burden which you have decided you must carry? God is telling you that you do not have to. You do not have to carry it at all; cast it all unto him and he will give you rest. He is the Rock of Ages and He wants to give you rest. Give all your burdens up to Him and have rest.

Chapter 15

STOOP DOWN

God's Vessels: Jerome Cofield

GOD CAN BLESS YOU AMID THE FLAMES. In the early '90s, my wife and I lost everything we owned in a devastating house fire. I will never forget that day; as the firefighters were trying to put the fire out, neighbors and people from the community began to come together in our yard. So many people stopped by and said all the right things; things that we needed to hear at that moment, such as, "everything is going to be ok", "we're praying for you" and, "if you need anything just let us know", and we embraced the comforting words.

In the middle of it all, I saw a car turn into our driveway, and Mrs. Edith Atkinson, got out of her car, and when I walked over to speak with her, I noticed a boy of about eleven or twelve years old in the back seat of her car. I did not even know his name then, but I do remember that he had hearing aids on. This young man pointed at the fire and then he pointed at me, and Mrs. Atkinson said, "Yes, that's who I was telling you that his house was on fire". He pointed a second time at the fire, then at me, and again, Mrs. Atkinson said "yes baby, that's the man I told you his house was on fire". Then, an amazing thing happened, the young man stooped in the backseat of the car and unlaced his shoes, took them off and handed them to me out of the window of the car. This young man did not say, "If you need anything, let me know"; the flames of the fire dictated and indicated that I did need something, and he gave me what he could. This young man came that day, operating in, and under the same Principle, Promise and Provision that God gave Abraham in Genesis 12:2 when He said, "I will bless you so that you will be a blessing", and because I know who I am and I know my self-worth, wherever that young man is today, I know he is truly blessed by God, because one of the fastest ways to get elevated by God is to stoop down first, in His presence. That is what he did in the backseat of Mrs. Edith Atkinson's car: he stooped down and came up with a blessing in his hands, and to this day, I am grateful.

Always ask God to give you more than enough so that you can always be a blessing to others. I have recently learned that the young man's name is Kerry Dunson, a well-respected and hardworking man of God, who still shines as a beacon of God's love.

#StoopDown
#WalkInYourAuthority
#GiveAndItShallBeGiven
#30YearsInTheWilderness

Author's Comments

What an empathetic young boy! God indeed, gave him the blessings and the wisdom to use his blessing to bless others. He saw a dire situation, and he did what he could, with what he had. Brethren, how often do we look to bless others with our blessings? Do you count your blessings? Do you seek ways to bless others when you are blessed? Remember that God's blessings in your life are the seeds that you sow into other people's lives. This young man, Kerry, in a fire disaster that saw Jerome possibly lose everything, gave what he could – his shoes – as evidence of God's love for us.

Let us become beacons of God's love. Let us be the light in a world full of darkness. Matthew 5:13-16 says, "you are the salt of the earth...you are the light of the world". Saints, we have been given the mandate and rights to be the salt of the earth. Let us take our rightful place in the world and shine the light of God's love to all peoples. May His Grace be with us.

Chapter 16

GOD'S UNFAILING LOVE

God Vessel: Clara Brown

IF IT HAD NOT BEEN FOR THE LORD ON MY side, where would I be? I love this scripture, Romans 5:8: "But God commendeth his love toward us: while we were sinners, Christ died for us". I am so grateful and honored to be among the living. If it were not for God's mercy and His grace, I would not be here. God tells us in Jeremiah 29:11, "for I know the plans and thoughts that I have towards you, saith the Lord, thoughts of peace and not of evil, to give you an expected end".

I have been in the world, of the world, been in the wrong places. Once, at night, I was in the wrong place – I could have easily got a shot to the head there! But God spared my life. He allowed me to get out of that situation. Now, that was love. Another night, when I was in the world, a gun was pointed at me, point blank, but the shooter did not pull the trigger. I walked away from that situation as well. There have been many other similar situations that I have experienced, and that God has intervened and saved me from. God did not let me taste death, even when it seemed inevitable. Why? Because he had a plan, a destiny, and an assignment for me to accomplish. A glorious conclusion: I am so delighted to know my God. I am alive only because He wants it so.

Author's Comments

Hallelujah! The enemy comes to steal, kill, and destroy. The enemy made many attempts on the life of my spiritual mother Clara, but, like Daniel in the Den, the Lord removed every threat to the life of his servant. Like the lions could not devour Daniel, so the would-be shooters could not pull the trigger. Even though Clara had many close calls God would not allow it to be. (2 Timothy 4:18 The Lord will rescue me from every evil deed and bring me safely into his heavenly kingdom. To him be the glory forever and ever. Amen.) Clara is truly God's own favored, a living promise that God never forsakes his people. God is the same God today, as He always has been. He is ever faithful to those who call on His name. His banner over us is love, and He never fails to prove this.

Chapter 17

GOD'S GRACE

God's Vessel: William Alston

HELLO, MY NAME IS WILLIAM ALSTON, and my story has many layers, dating back to before my birth.

The very first miracle of God's presence in my life was when I was born with my umbilical cord wrapped securely around my neck, which, under normal circumstances, would have spelled death for a fetus, but I survived. As a child, I recounted certain events, including this, to my mother, even though I had no way of knowing that they had taken place.

Throughout my childhood, I survived several near-death experiences, to be spared only by God's grace. My Aunt told me that I was here to do God's will. I did not understand why, but she said that it was important to God, and that He assigned me to do just that, His will. I never understood how, when I was young, I was able to see people I knew

97

who had died come back to visit me, clear as day. While they stood by my bed on the left topside, some would speak, while others would smile and walk away. As a young child, my grandmother told me she and my mother had this special gift as well. I was to never speak, but to only listen.

Throughout my young adult life, I have wrestled with my beliefs because of things I did not understand. I have witnessed death all around me, from holding a beautiful young lady's hand as she passed away from an accident, to people being shot footsteps away from me, and so I wonder, why me? Why did I survive? I have fallen asleep at the wheel and gone off a bridge, had countless accidents where my car ended up looking like a pretzel, and been involved in a misunderstanding with a former drug dealer who, years later, became a pastor, but who at the time, did not know me as I was new to the area. He had picked a fight with me and pulled a gun on me and was squeezing the trigger at my head, but with divine intervention, the gun did not fire. Years later, this man, who is now a Pastor, told me that God spared both our lives that night. I truly have no clue why I have been spared so many times throughout my life; I am just a regular guy who tries to treat everyone with respect because that is the way I was raised.

My last God's grace event happened on August 16, 2019, at 6:17am. I had just gotten off my shift. A co-worker had a flat tire, so I told him that I was going to pull up ahead and wait for him to put all his stuff back into his car, since he was unable to change the flat. We decided that maybe he could put enough air in the tire at the gas station up the street, so that he could make it home. So, I pulled ahead and parked, leaving my truck still running. My headlight looked like it was out, so I jumped out of the truck and tapped on the headlight. It came right on, and as it did so, my truck slammed into the reverse gear, catching me off guard. My first thought was that someone was stealing my truck, so my first reaction was to run after it. After I realized that no one was in it, I tried to stop it from hurting someone that was trying to get in their vehicle. As I tried to stop the truck, it knocked me down, rolled over my chest and nicked my head. After this attempt, I was able to immediately jump back up, trying to stop it once more, but it was then moving fast, and I got caught under it again. It rolled over my chest once more as it ran into the curb and finally stopped in the grass. I laid there in the street in no pain and did not hear anyone talk to me. I heard the Word asking me, "What do you want to do?" It was the most peaceful feeling that I have ever encountered. As I started to think about my wife and my family, I answered, "I want to stay". Immediately, I felt intense pain sweep across my body and envelope me. I was put into an ambulance, taken to a medical helicopter, and airlifted to a critical Intensive Care Unit. When I arrived, my prognosis was slim to none that I would survive. I heard the chaplain praying over me. I was able to hear and see everything. I was in the hospital for a week as every bone in my chest was broken. I had no internal bleeding injuries at all. My X-ray showed my chest cavity wrapping and cradling my heart. The surgeon assigned to me was blown away because with a vehicle rolling over you point-blank once, you are given only a 20% chance of survival, but with it rolling over you twice, you simply had no chance of survival. But there I was, alive and without any internal bleeding. My case was so shockingly rare that they recorded my recovery for study. I later walked out of the hospital, fully recovered from an impossible situation.

My final thoughts are these: all my blessings come from above. He is real and He will be there when you need him the most. Since my accident, I have been led to create a mentorship program for boys and young men. I believe God has put this purpose in my heart and in my life to save someone's son from the streets, who in turn will do God's work as well.

Author's Comments

An amazing testimony this was! It was beautiful until the end. God clearly had a purpose for William from even before he was formed in his mother's womb! William, in turn, understood that most of the happenings in his life were supernatural, and that he was sent here on Earth to do God's bidding. The piece about him being born with his umbilical cord wrapped around his neck, yet he was not stillborn is simply God being God. He was also blessed with the ability to see things others could not and was blessed with a supportive family. God plants his roses carefully.

William honored and obeyed God and always gave God his due praise because he knew he pulled through so many tough situations solely because God was leading him. Because William opened the eyes of his heart, he was able to communicate with the Holy Spirit, who asked him what he wanted to do, after he'd been steamrollered by his truck, TWICE!, and he chose to stay, for the love of his earthly family. Despite being steamrollered, he survived! The devil is powerless over us! William's doctors and surgeons were awe-struck and could not believe their eyes because his survival defied all logic and science. (1 Corinthians 1:25 says, "for the foolishness of God is wiser than human wisdom".) God's ways simply defy human logic. He does not act so man can understand. He does what he does as the true Living God so that man can see what he did and give him his due praise. Glory be to God! Amen!

Chapter 18

LED BY GOD

God's Vessel: Edith Atkinson

MY NAME IS EDITH ATKINSON, I AM excited to share my testimony about how God saved me, led me, and kept me as a single mother of four at the time. In the early 80's one night after a long shift at work, I came home, and I felt like I couldn't get in my room fast enough. I was sick of the world and all it had to offer. I had enough! I wanted Jesus! I got down on my knees and prayed. I asked God to forgive me for my sins. I cried and prayed. I laid it all down that night. I remember that prayer so vividly, it will always be etched on the forefront of my heart because I meant every single word. Dear Lord if it takes me being alone to be a Christian I will. I will do whatever it takes. (Heb 10:22 Let us draw near with a sincere heart in full assurance of faith, having our hearts sprinkled clean from an evil conscience and our bodies washed with pure water.)

Beloved how many of you know that is all it took was a sincere heart. That very night I was born again. Glory hallelujah! Right there in my bedroom God changed me from my old nature and he made me new. I started to see things differently, I felt free, the chains were lifted and everything that was attached unattached that night.

In days to come I began praying about a way to get my family in a better home. The home we had down south was built in the 70's and it was without running water and an indoor bath. It is not what I wanted for us. (Proverbs 29:18 Where there is no vision the people perish, but he that keeps the law happy is he). Friends do not ever stop dreaming, reach High, even if you do not reach the intended goal, you will get close. My oldest sister lived out west in California. I started to think perhaps moving there would give us the new start we needed. I was conflicted in my mind. I had a good job in nursing, I had a good support system with my family all living so closely together, but it did not change my living conditions. So, I continued to pray, asking God to guide me. Give me a sign. The very first vision I had was God giving me the okay to go to California. After working the 2nd shift one night and as tired as I could be, I finally made it home. I took a huge sigh of relief to be a few steps away from a lil bit of relaxation. I made my way up a few steps, keys already in hand. As soon as I opened the front door directly in front of me, I looked upon a vision unveiling the most beautiful green palm trees I have ever seen! The sun shined so beautifully brighter than a sunny warm day in spring. It all happened so quickly but there was no doubt in my mind what I just saw and why I saw it. I felt confident that it was my sign that relocating to California was indeed a good move for my family. (Psalm 37:23 The steps of a good man are ordered by the Lord.)

When I called my sister Frances about the idea of the kids and I relocating, she was ecstatic! Yes, you all are more than welcomed, when are you coming? The questions went on. However, my mom, sister, and other family members were not so happy about the idea. But after sitting down with them and sharing my heart and my reasons they seem to let up a bit. I began to save and pre-pare to relocate to California. I was confident that God would be with us every step of the way, and he was. We had a nice ride there. The kids got to see bigger cities and mountains as we traveled. We had a good time together. I can tell you one of the many things that made our trip was having obedient respectful kids. They really stuck close to me out there at the bus stations and restaurants. The day we arrived in California is a day to remember. My sister and I embraced for a long time as my nieces, nephews and my kids were all meeting for the first time. My sister cooked a yellow chocolate cake for the kids and one of the best meals. We laughed and talked all night. I was not there 2 days before I got busy getting familiar with the city life. I registered the kids for school and started looking at affordable housing for us. Even though my sister's doors were opened for us to live there, I knew I wanted my own place for my family. Would you believe not even a month being there God opened so many doors for us. A three-bedroom apartment became available directly across the street from where my sister lived. I was blessed with the apartment and I was also blessed to become assistant manager of the complex. God had certainly opened doors for us. (1 Corinthians 16:9 for a wide door for effective work has opened to me and there are many adversaries.)

After about 6 months of living in our new place, I was blessed to buy us a car. Even though it was the norm to ride buses, it was not the norm for me. No, it was not a brand new car but it rode just fine. I cannot tell you how blessed we were to be a blessing to others. I was on fire for God and every chance I had I witnessed to as many people as I could. I had not been saved that long, but the Holy Spirit would always give me the words for each individual I witnessed. For whoever may read my testimony, if you take anything from my experience please take the fact that the same thing God did for me, he can and will do for you. Trust him.

Authors Comments

This testimony happens to be one of my favorites! One of the main reasons is because I witnessed and lived it too. This faithful servant Mrs. Edith Atkinson is my Queen, my mother. Her example and the things she taught me by the way she lived is the examples of faithfulness I stand on today as a mother and wife. My mother introduced us to Christ at an early age. I am so thankful for the privilege to be her daughter. Saints you cannot go wrong with the Lord. He can save you right where you are.

Chapter 19

GOD DON'T MAKE MISTAKES

God's Vessel: Demecia Lewis

I RECALL BACK IN 2003 RECEIVING THE worst news any mother would dread to hear during a routine ultrasound. As I lay on the table anxiously awaiting to see the rapid heartbeat of our unborn baby during the exam, the doctor seemed concerned as she continued to search for her heartbeat and to my dismay, she located her heart but there was no beat. My baby girl had passed away before I could ever see her beautiful little face. I was totally devastated and not expecting to receive this unexpected loss. I went through a deep depression. Through prayers and support of my loved ones, God brought me out. Although I grieved for a long time, I began to eventually accept that God does not make mistakes because He is the Creator. I never questioned him although my pain was intense. I know that God has a plan for my life, and I had to stand firm on that belief although I struggled at the time.

It was not until a few years later that I under-stood His plan even more when I received diagnoses of multiple sclerosis and fibromyalgia. I was fortu-nate that my sons were a little older and more inde-pendent because I had countless days stuck in bed with pain or even worse in a hospital bed. I do know that if I had a two-year-old daughter at that time it would have been difficult for me. Nevertheless, we do all we can within us to stay strong in our faith. Fibromyalgia and Multiple Sclerosis (MS) just the diagnoses alone had me in great fear from the very beginning. The first thing I did when I got home was get on the computer and researched everything, I could find about MS. Even though the doctors explained in the short amount of time they give you during your appointment it is not even close to enough time after hearing something like this. I read so many things that caused me to fear. So many questions raced through my mind. Would I lose my ability to walk? would I lose my eyesight? would I be able to raise my sons and continue to enjoy playing with them? I have always been very hands on with our children. Everything from jumping on the trampoline to riding bikes, playing basketball you name it We did it. Not only was that a fear but I enjoyed cooking and taking care of my family. I did not work outside the home after we started to have our children. I was so blessed to be home and take care of them. At the time we were a military family. Though we did not make financially what we wanted, it was always enough. The one thing I quickly learned was that fear is the opposite of faith. I absolutely could not do both. I was going to have to trust God and stand on his promise that he would never leave me nor forsake me. Or stay in a dark unfruitful state of mourning and sadness. Thankfully, I was reared from a family of believers, though we lived in different cities at the time it did not minimize the impact of their prayers over me and their encouraging words of support. My husband being a man of faith always reminded me of who I am in Christ, that God is a healer, He is faithful, and He needed me whole because I have work to do. He spoke life to me during MS flareups. They were so hard to bear. The steroid infusions they used to treat the flare ups was a nightmare. Causing weight gain, terrible dreams, hallucinations. I am so thankful it has been over 15 years now and I have not had flareups severe enough to have to be on steroid infusions. A question many ask themselves in the privacy of their hearts, Am I ever going to be healed?

This was a question I asked myself many times as well about my diagnoses of MS and fibromyalgia. Just from the experiences that I have shared with you, I know that God is a healer. I am so very thankful to share with you the good news that I received after I had taken an MRI test. My neurologist told me that the lesions in my brain had decreased in ways that he has never seen before and that the decision was mine to start taking the medication to treat my earlier diagnosis. Saints, I remember that day so vividly because my heart filled with joy. Does this mean that I am healed from these things? By faith, yes. I must walk by faith and not by sight. Even when similar symptoms arise that is familiar. I still must believe. One thing I realize the enemy is a deceiver of the brethren. He is also an imitator, so it is not unusual at all for him to try to attack us with familiar symptoms. One thing I know it is not God on one side and satan on the other. The enemy do not have enough power or authority to be placed on the opposite side of our great sovereign God, God created him. Remember he was once an angel that was kicked out of heaven. The word of God say I saw satan fall like lighting! Can you imagine how solid and fast that fall was? Friends do not live in fear. Trust God totally. He will not fail. He will not give up on you, his love for you will not change because you fall. Get back up, repent, and turn away from that sin and live.

ACKNOWLEDGEMENT

I am searching for the words to express how thankful I am to be blessed with my husband, *Shawn Lewis,* of 23 years. This Man of God has stood by me through every trial and test. Supported and encouraged every business venture. He has celebrated with me, prayed with me, held me during my storms. My husband, My prayer partner, My lover, My friend for life thank you for giving me all of you.

PRAYER OF SALVATION

Father, I am a sinner, and I ask You to forgive me of my sins. Cleanse me with Your blood and wash me from all unrighteousness. I believe that Jesus died on the cross for my sins, and on the third day, You raised Him from the dead. Father, I ask You to fill me with Your Holy Spirit now and write my name in the Lamb's Book of Life. I give my entire life to You from this day on. In Jesus' name, I pray, amen.

If you confess with your mouth the Lord Jesus and believe in your heart that God has raised Him from the dead, you will be saved. For with the heart one believes unto righteousness, and with the mouth confession is made unto salvation.

(Romans 10:9-10 NKJV).

BAPTISM OF THE HOLY SPIRIT

Heavenly Father, I plead the Blood of my Lord and Savior Jesus Christ over me and I thank You for the most wonderful gift of salvation. Lord Jesus You promised me another gift, the gift of the Holy Spirit. So, I ask You Lord Jesus, to baptize and fill me in and with Your Holy Spirit, just as You filled Your disciples on the day of Pentecost. Christ Jesus, I am one of your disciple(s), filled with the Holy Spirit just as Your disciples. I will try to do what You tell me to do, I forgive all those who have ever caused me pain, trauma, shock, harm, rejection, or shame, and I ask You to forgive them. I also ask You to forgive me for holding a judgement against them.

Thank You Lord Jesus that I am filled with Your Holy Spirit and begin to speak with other tongues, as the Spirit gives me utterance.
(Acts 2:4 KJV).

CPSIA information can be obtained
at www.ICGtesting.com
Printed in the USA
LVHW080952201220
674416LV00013BA/1278